To Mum with much love from Janie xx
Happy Birthday & many happy memories
6th Dec. 1989.

MURDER, MURDER, POLIS!

Glasgow Street Songs
and Games Rhymes

MURDER, MURDER, POLIS!

Glasgow Street Songs
and Games Rhymes

Compiled by

MAUREEN SINCLAIR

Illustrations by Margot Wallace

THE RAMSAY HEAD PRESS EDINBURGH

© 1986 Maureen Sinclair

First published in 1986 by
The Ramsay Head Press
15 Gloucester Place
Edinburgh EH3 6EE

ISBN 0 902859 91 9

Printed in Scotland by
W. M. Bett Ltd, Tillicoultry

CONTENTS

"One two three, Ma mammy caught a flea"

Glasgow Street Songs

This is a collection of songs and rhymes which have been sung by Glasgow children for many years.

These songs once echoed throughout the streets and back courts of Glasgow as the children amused and entertained themselves, although indeed, many of them were sung by children all over the country.

Now the streets are strangely quiet. No longer can we hear the strains of 'Ali bali bee' or 'Ma maw's a million-aire' reverberating in the distance at the end of a long summer day. As the old tenements disappear and the high rise flats and housing schemes emerge, the only sounds we are likely to hear as today's youngsters enter-tain themselves are the latest pop tunes blaring from expensive 'ghetto blasters' or the screech of brakes from BMX bikes.

As these songs have meant so much to so many people in the past it would be a great pity for them to be lost in history. It is for this reason I have tried to capture as many as possible in one collection in the hope that they will bring back many happy memories and help to rekindle the joys of youth to the children of yesterday.

Last night there wis murder at the chip shop
A wee dug stole a haddy bone
A big dug tried tae get it aff him
So Ah hit him wi' a big tattie scone
Ah shouted on ma auntie Sarah
Ma auntie Sarah wisnae in
Ah peeped through a hole in the windae
An' Ah shouted auntie Sarah are ye in?
Her teeth were lyin' on the table
Her hair wis hangin' oot the bed
Ah nearly burst ma sides wi laughin'
When Ah saw her screwin' aff her wooden leg.

Ma maw says Ah've tae go
Wi' ma faither's dinner – o
Champit totties stewin' steak
An' a wee bit currant cake
Ah came tae a river
Ah couldnae get across
Ah paid ten bob fur an' auld scabby horse
Ah jumped on his back
His bones gave a crack
Ah had tae wait till the boat came back
The boat came back we a' jumped in
The boat capsized and we a' fell in
Singin' don't be weary try an' be cheery
Don't be weary cos we're A' goin' hame.

Murder murder polis
Three stairs up
The wummin in the middle door
Hit me wi' a cup
Ma head's a' blood
An' ma face is a' cut
Murder murder polis
Three stairs up
Send fur the doctor
The doctor widnae come
Send for the ambulance
Run run run.

Last night Ah got an' awfu' hammerin'
Who frae? frae wee Geordie Cameron
Whit fur? fur calling' his daddy greasy beard
Ah'll tell the bobbies in the mornin'.

Ma maw's a millionaire
Wid ye believe it
Blue eyes an' curly hair
Wid ye believe it
Sittin' among the eskimoes
Playing' a game o' dominoes
Ma maw's a millionaire.

Last night Ah went tae the pictures
Ah took a front seat at the back
Ah fell frae the pit tae the gallery
An broke a front bone at the back
Ah wummin she gave me some chocolates
Ah ate them an' gave her them back
She said Ah wis comin' on funny
An' gave me a big lassie slap.

Doh ray me when Ah wis wee ✓
Ah used tae peel the totties
Noo Ah'm big an' Ah can jig
An' Ah can play wi' the loddies
Ma faither bought me a wee wee hoose
Tae keep me away frae the loddies
The hoose fell in an' Ah fell oot
An' Ah fell in wi' the loddies.

Kilty kilty cauld bum ✓
Couldnae play a drum
He lifted up his petticoat
An' showed his dirty bum
His dirty bum was dirty
He showed it tae the queen
The queen wis disappointed
An' jagged it wi' a peen.

Up an' doon the hoose
Tae catch a mickey moose
If ye catch it by the tail
Hang it up on a rusty nail
Send for the cook
Tae make a bowl o' soup
Hurrah boys hurrah boys
How d'ye like ma soup?
Ah like it very well
But only for the smell
Hurrah boys hurrah boys
How d'ye like ma soup?

Paddy on the railway ✓
Pickin up stones
Along came an engine
An' broke Paddy's bones
Oh says Paddy
That's no' fair
Oh says the engine man
Ye shouldnae hae been there.

One two three ✓
Ma mammy caught a flea
She put it in the sugar bowl
An' took it tae her tea.

Oor wee school's the best wee school ✓
The best wee school in Glesca
The only thing that's wrang wi' it
Is the baldy headed maister
He goes tae the pub on a Saturday night
He goes tae church on Sunday
An' prays tae God tae gie him strength
Tae belt the weans on Monday.

The bell the bell the B – E – L ✓
Tell the teacher Ah'm no' well
If ye're late shut the gate
The bell the bell the B – E – L.

Ma mammy says tae me
Wid ye like a cup o' tea?
Ah says no no Ah like cocoa
Down in the glen
She took me by the hand
All the way tae Barrowland
Ah says no no Ah like cocoa
Down in the glen.

Wee chookie birdie toh loh loh
Laid an egg on the windae sill
The windae sill began tae crack
Wee chookie birdie quack quack quack.

Ali bali ali bali bee ✓
Sittin' on yer mammy's knee
Greetin' fur a wee bawbee
Tae buy some coulter's candy
Coulter's candy a penny a lump
That's the stuff tae make ye jump
If ye jump yer sure tae fall
Ockey Cockey that's it all.

Ah'm no' hairy Mary Ah'm yer maw
Ah'm no' hairy Mary Ah'm yer maw
Ah'm no' hairy Mary Ah'm no' hairy Mary
Ah'm no' hairy Mary Ah'm yer maw.

Skinny malinky long legs ✓
Big banana feet
Went tae the pictures
An' couldnae find a seat
When the picture started
Skinny malinky farted
Skinny malinky long legs
Big banana feet.

Hey Jock ma cuddy ✓
Ma cuddy's o'er the dyke
An' if ye touch ma cuddy
Ma cuddy'll gie ye a bite.

The weans have gone tae Balloch
Wi' ribbons in their hair
Tae the bonnie banks of Loch Lomond
Dear God we'll all be there
Teacher dear teacher
Dae ye know what Ah have done?
Ma pastry's fell intae Loch Lomond
Will ye gie me another wee bun (bun bun)
Ah'll remember St Patrick's excursion
Until I'm a hundred and one (one one).

Does yer maw drink wine
Does she drink it a' the time
Does she ever get the feelin'
That she's gonni hit the ceilin'
Does yer maw drink wine?
Does yer maw drink gin?
Does she drink it oot a tin?
Does she ever get the feelin'
That she's gonni hit the ceilin'
Does yer maw drink gin?

Wee Jeannie's a smasher
A face like a tottie masher
A nose like a pickled onion
An' big smelly feet.

Ah merried a wife oh then oh then
Ah merried a wife oh then oh then
Ah merried a wife
An' she hit me wi' a knife
Oh the world must be comin' tae an end
Ah sent her fur butter oh then oh then
Ah sent her fur butter oh then oh then
Ah sent her fur butter
An' she fell in the gutter
Oh the world must be comin' tae an end
Ah sent her fur cheese oh then oh then
Ah sent her fur cheese oh then oh then
Ah sent her fur cheese
An' she fell an' skint her knees
Oh the world must be comin' tae an end
Ah sent her fur bread oh then oh then
Ah sent her fur bread oh then oh then
Ah sent her fur bread
An' she drapped doon deid
Oh the world must be comin' tae an end.

Me an' ma granny an' a whale lot mair
Kicked up a rammy on the wash hoose stair
Alang came a polisman an' said who's there
Jist me an' ma granny an' a whale lot mair.

Tell tale tit yer mammy cannae knit ✓
Yer daddy cannae go tae bed withoot a dummy tit.

Oh Mary oh Mary are ye no' comin' oot?
Yer laud's at the corner
He's walkin' aboot
His hauns in his pocket
His shirt's hangin' oot
Oh Mary oh Mary are ye no' comin' oot?
Oh Mary oh Mary oh Mary come quick
Yer laud's wi' the polis
He's goin' tae the nick
He stole three rolls
As hard as a brick
Oh Mary oh Mary oh Mary come quick.

Ma wee laud's a sailor ✓
He works in Maryhill
He gets his pay on a Friday night
An' buys a hauf a gill
He goes tae church on Sunday
A half an hour late
He pulls the buttons aff his shirt
An' puts them in the plate.

Ha ha ha hee hee hee
Three wee monkies up a tree
One fell doon an' skint his knee
Ha ha ha hee hee hee.

Greasy beard a penny a yerd
A ha'penny a wee bit longer.

Wee MacGreegor he's like a nigger
His name was even on the irn bru
He wears a tammy tae please his mammy
Wee MacGreegor Greegor Greegor Greegor do.

Oh the bonnie wee barra's mine
It disnae belang tae O'Hara
The barra broke at ten o' clock
An' Ah lost ma hurl in the barra.

Felix had a baby
Had a baby boy
He wis like his daddy
They only called him Paddy
Paddy died an' Felix cried
And all the people laughed
Ha ha ha hee hee hee hee
Three wee monkies up a tree
But he kept on walkin'
He kept on walkin' still.

Mrs MacLean she had a wee wean
An' she didnae know how tae nurse it
She gave it tae me
An' Ah gave it some tea
An' it's bonnie wee belly bursted.

Oh Peter the taliman
Chippy no' ready
Wait a wee minute
Ah'll no be long.

If you should see a big fat wummin
Standin' at the corner bummin
That's ma mammy.
If you should see her wearin' glasses
Smiling at each one that passes
That's ma mammy.

Old mother Reilly at the pawn shop door
A baby in her arms and a bundle on the floor
She asked for ten and she only got four
She nearly took the hinges off the pawn shop door.

No' last night but the night before
Three wee beggars came to my door
One had a fiddle one had a drum
And one had a pancake stuck to his bum.

How wid ye like tae be me?
How wid ye like tae be me?
A lump o' fat stuck in ma hat
How wid ye like tae be me?

Sugarally watter black as the lum ✓
A' get a pin an' we'll a' get some.

Open the gates and let me in sir
I am soaking to the skin sir
Open the gates and let me in sir
Early in the morning.

Hallelujah slice the dumpling
Hallelujah amen
Hallelujah slice the dumpling
Hallelujah amen.

Jenny Myer blow the fire puff puff puff
When she sits on her husband's knee snuff snuff snuff
When she goes to bed at night huff huff huff.

Coco Bendy had a wife
She was awfu' dandy
She fell in beneath the bed
An' tumbled o'er the chanty
Coco Bendy he came in
An' smelt an' awfu' stink
He went in below the bed
An' had a fizzy drink.

Whit's yer name?
Baldy Bain.
Stick yer nose in an aeroplane
An' don't come back tae me again.

Circle Games Rhymes

Most of the circle games rhymes have a similar theme.

A group of children gather round circle fashion and sing and act out the words of the song.

Sometimes one child goes into the centre of the circle and acts out the words of the song whilst all the others stand around clapping hands and singing the song.

When the song is ended the child in the centre chooses someone to take her place, and the song is repeated.

This process is repeated until each child has had her turn in the centre of the circle. Then another song is sung.

"Ring a ring o' roses, A cuppa cuppa shell"

Hot peas and barley-o barley-o barley-o ✓
Hot peas and barley-o
Sugary cakes and candy
This is the way the teacher stands
This is the way she folds her arms
This is the way she claps her hands
And this is the way she dances.

I've got the legs like Betty Grable
I've got the figure like Marilyn Monroe
I've got the hair like Ginger Rodgers
And the face I do not know
I've got the eyes like Charlie Chaplin
They shine for you alone
Yes I've got the legs like Betty Grable
And the figure like Marilyn Monroe.

Bee baw babbity babbity babbity ✓
Bee baw babbity a lassie or a wee laudie
Ah widnae hae a lassie-o a lassie-o a lassie-o
Ah widnae hae a lassie-o
Ah'd rather hae a wee laudie.

Hard up kick the can
Jeannie Smith's got a man
If ye'd like tae know his name
His name is Johnny Thompson.

Nellie McSwiggan got tossed oot the jiggin'
For liftin' her leg too high
All of a sudden a big black puddin'
Came flyin' through the air
Oh wha saw the kilties comin'
Wha saw them gang awa'
Wha saw the kilties comin'
Sailin' doon the Broomlielaw
Some o' them had tartan troosers
Some o' them had nane at a'
Some o' them had tartan troosers
Sailin' doon the Broomielaw.

Ma name is MacNamara
Ah'm the leader o' the band
Ma wife is Betty Grable
She's the fairest in the land
She can dance and she can sing
And she can show a leg
The only thing she cannae dae
Is fry ma ham and egg
Ta ra ra ra ta ra ra ra a
The only thing she cannae dae
Is fry ma ham and egg.

Salome Salome you should see Salome
Hands up there skirts in the air
You should see Salome
Swing it swing it you should see her swing it
Hands up there skirts in the air
You should see her swing it.

My girl's a corker she's a New Yorker
I'd give her anything to keep her in style
She's got a pair of legs just like two boiled eggs
That's where all my money goes
Oompah oompah oompah pah
Oompah pah pah oompah pah
Oompah oompah oompah pah
That's where all my money goes.

I'm Shirley Temple and I've got curly hair
I've got dimples and I wear my clothes to there
I'm not yet able to do my Betty Grable
I'm Shirley Temple and I've got curly hair.

We're the three wee galous girls
And if you'd like to know
And if you pick the fairest one
You'll have to pick us a'
With a rishy tishy petticoat
A rishy tishy-o
A rishy tishy petticoat
A rishy tishy-o.

Down in the jungle where nobody goes
A big fat mama sat a-washing her clothes
With a rub a dub here
And a rub a dub there
That's the way she washes her clothes.

Down in yonder meadow where the green grass grows
Where Mary Wilson bleaches all her clothes
She sang and she sang and she sang so sweet
She sang Jimmy Jones across the street
She huddled and she cuddled and she sat upon his knee
Saying my dear Jimmy I hope you will agree
Agree agree I hope you will agree
Saying my dear Jimmy I hope you will agree
Mary made a dumpling she made it awful nice
She cut it up in slices and gave us all a slice
Saying taste it taste it don't say no
For tomorrow is my wedding day and I must go.

Two little sandy girls ✓
Sitting by the shore
Crying weeping very very sore
Stand up Mary and wipe away your tears
And who's the one you love the best
And that's Jeannie dear.

I have a bonnet trimmed with blue
Do you wear it? Yes I do
I always wear it when I can
Going to the ball with my young man
My young man has gone to sea
When he comes back he will marry me
Tip to the heel and tip to the toe
That's the way the polka goes.

When grandmama met grandpapa
They danced the minuet
The minuet was too slow
They danced a quick step
With a heel toe heel toe
Give it a kick
Heel toe heel toe
Give it a kick
Heel toe heel toe
Give it a kick
That's the way to do it.

Red cheeks and roses roses roses
Red cheeks and roses Y – O – U
I met him at a dance hall dance hall dance hall
I met him at a dance hall Y – O – U
Red cheeks and roses roses roses
Red cheeks and roses Y – O – U
This is the one that I love I love I love
This is the one that I love Y – O – U
Red cheeks and roses roses roses
Red cheeks and roses Y – O – U.

My mummy told me if I was goody
That she would buy me a rubber dolly
But auntie told her I kissed a soldier
Now she won't buy me a rubber dolly
Three six nine the goose drank wine
The monkey chewed tobacco on the street car line
The line broke the monkey got choked
And they all went to heaven in a little row boat.

Keep the sunny side up up
And the other side one two
See those soldiers marching along
See those sailors singing their song
Bend down and touch your toes
Just like the Eskimoes
Bend down and touch your shins
Just like the Indians
Bend down and touch your knees
Just like the Japanese
But keep the sunny side up.

Who shaved the barber the barber the barber
Who shaved the barber
The barber shaved himself
Who put on his waistcoat his waistcoat his waistcoat
Who put on his waistcoat
He put it on himself.
Catch him by the waistcoat
The jaicket the overcoat
Tell him he's a billygoat
And throw him doon the stairs.

There was a farmer had a dog
His name was Bobby Bingo
B – I – N – G – O   B – I – N – G – O
B – I – N – G –O
His name was Bobby Bingo.

I'm a sailor home from sea
To see if you will marry me
If you will marry arry arry arry
If you will marry me.

So you're a sailor home from sea
To see if you can marry me
Well I won't marry arry arry arry
I won't marry you.

I will give you a silver spoon
To feed your baby in the afternoon
If you will marry arry arry arry
If you will marry me.

> I don't want a silver spoon
> To feed my baby in the afternoon
> And I won't marry arry arry arry
> I won't marry you.

I will give you a bouncing ball
That bounces from the kitchen into the hall
If you will marry arry arry arry
If you will marry me.

> I don't want a bouncing ball
> That bounces from the kitchen into the hall
> And I won't marry arry arry arry
> I won't marry you.

I will give you the keys of the chest
And all the money that I possess
If you will marry arry arry arry
If you will marry me.

> I will take the keys of the chest
> And all the money that you possess
> But I won't marry arry arry arry
> I won't marry you.

Ha ha ha you're awful funny
You don't want me but you want my money
Well I won't marry arry arry arry
I won't marry you.

Ring a ring o' roses
A cuppa cuppa shell
The duck's away to Hamilton
To buy a new bell
If you don't tak' it
Ah'll tak' it to masel
A ring a ring o' roses
A cuppa cuppa shell.

I'm a bow legged chicken
I'm a knock kneed hen
Never been so happy
Since I don't know when
I walk with a wiggle
And a giggle and a gog
Doin' the Tennessee wig wog
Put your toes together
Your knees apart
Bend your back
Get ready to start
Flap your elbows just for luck
Then you wiggle and you woggle
Like a baby duck.

I sent a letter to my love ✓
And on the way I dropped it
I dropped it once
I dropped it twice
I dropped it three times over
Over over in and out the clover
Over over in and out the clover.

The farmer wants a wife ✓
The farmer wants a wife
Ee-o my daddy-o
The farmer wants a wife.
The wife wants a child
The wife wants a child
Ee-o my daddy-o
The wife wants a child.
The child wants a nurse
The child wants a nurse
Ee-o my daddy-o
The child wants a nurse.
The nurse wants a dog
The nurse wants a dog
Ee-o my daddy-o
The nurse wants a dog.
The dog wants a bone
The dog wants a bone
Ee-o my daddy-o
The dog wants a bone.
The bone won't break
The bone won't break
Ee-o my daddy-o
The bone won't break.

In and out those dusty bluebells √
In and out those dusty bluebells
In and out those dusty bluebells
I am the master.
Tipper ipper apper on my shoulder
Tipper ipper apper on my shoulder
Tipper ipper apper on my shoulder
I am the master.
Follow me the master says
Follow me the master says
Follow me the master says
I am the master.

Who'll come in tae ma wee ring? √
Ma wee ring, ma wee ring?
Who'll come in tae ma wee ring
Tae make it a wee bit bigger?
Ah'll come in tae your wee ring
Your wee ring, your wee ring
Ah'll come in tae your wee ring
Tae make it a wee bit bigger.
Who'll come in tae oor wee ring
Oor wee ring, oor wee ring?
Who'll come in tae oor wee ring
Tae make it a wee bit bigger?
Ah'll come in tae your wee ring
Your wee ring, your wee ring
Ah'll come in tae your wee ring
Tae make it a wee bit bigger.
Etc. . . .

" Up skalla doon skalla Back skalla roon skalla"

Ball Game Rhymes

The ball game rhymes are sung or spoken as the child bounces a ball against a wall and catches it. Sometimes two balls are used which requires a little more skill and practice.

If the ball drops and the child fails to catch it she is 'out' and it is the next player's turn.

If the words of the song include the word 'up' the ball is thrown up against the wall. If the word 'down' is included the ball is bounced down on the ground. If there are numbers or counting in the rhyme the ball is caught with one hand.

Whoever finishes the rhyme with the least number of 'turns' is the winner.

My mother's a queen
And my father's a king
I'm a little princess
And you're a dirty wee thing
It's not because you're dirty
It's not because you're clean
It's because you've got the chickenpox
And measles in between
If my mother knew
That I played with you
She'd put me over the bannister
And this is what she'd do
One two three o-leary
Four five six o-leary
Seven eight nine o-leary
Ten o-leary postman.

Away up in Scotland
The land of the Scotch
There lives a wee lassie
I love very much
Her name is Susannah
But where is she now?
She's up in the highlands
A-milking the cow.

Cobbler cobbler mend my shoe
Have it done by half past two
Half past two is far too late
Have it done by half past eight.

Early in the morning before eight o'clock
You should hear the postman knock
Up jumps Mary running to the door
With a one a letter two a letter
Three a letter four.

Tommy had a gun and the gun was loaded
Tommy pulled the trigger and the gun exploded
No more Tommy no more gun
No more damage to be done

Now the war is over
Hitler is dead
He wants to go to heaven
With a crown upon his head
But the Lord says no
He'll have to go below
There's only room for Churchill
And his wee banjo.

Mary had a baby
And she called him sunny Jim
She put him in the bath tub
To see if he could swim
He drank all the water
He ate all the soap
He died last night
With a bubble in his throat.

When I was young I had no sense
I thought I'd go to sea
I stepped upon a Chinaman's ship
And the Chinaman said to me
Up skalla doon skalla
Back skalla roon skalla
That's what the Chinaman said to me.

Rabbie Burns was born in Ayr
Now he stands in George's Square
If you'd like to see him there
Just jump on the bus and pay your fare
A penny, tuppence, thruppence,
fourpence, fivepence, sixpence,
sevenpence, eightpence, ninepence,
tenpence, elevenpence, a shilling.

Stop says the red light
Go says the green
Wait says the amber light
Blinking in between
That's what they say
And that's what they mean
We all must obey them
Even the queen.

The wind the wind the wind blows high
The rain comes tumbling from the sky
Mary Smith says she'll die
If she doesn't get the boy
With the big blue eye.
Annie Thomson says she loves him
All the girls are fighting for him
He's the prettiest boy in Glasgow
Pray pray pray for him.

Korky the cat thinks he's smart
Because he put a penny in the old man's hat
If you haven't got a penny
A ha'penny will do
If you haven't got a ha'penny
A farthing will do
If you haven't got a farthing
God Bless You.

Salvation army free from sin
Went to heaven in a corn mutton tin
The corn mutton tin began to smell
Salvation army went to hell.

Wee Sam a piece on jam
Went to London in a pram
The pram broke what a joke
Wee Sam a piece on jam.

Mrs McGuire sat on the fire
The fire was too hot
She sat on the pot
The pot was too wide
She sat on the Clyde
And all the wee fishes
Ran up her backside.

Mrs Simpson lives by the shore
She has daughters three and four
The oldest one is twenty four
Married to the boy next door

Mrs White got a fright
In the middle of the night
She saw a ghost eating toast
Halfway up the lamp post.

Mrs Brown went to town
With her knickers hanging down.

Mrs Red went to bed
In the morning she was dead.

P.K. chewing gum a penny a packet ✓/
First you chew it then you crack it
Then you stick it to your jacket
P.K. chewing gum a penny a packet.

The big ship was leaving Bombay for today
Back to old Erin's isle so they say
Mary was standing with tears in her eyes
Along came a sailor with two big brown eyes
Singing Mary O Mary be mine
I'll send you a sweet valentine
And he turned round and kissed her
And said he would miss her
O Mary it won't be for long so long.

Dan Dan the funny wee man ✓/
Washed his face in the frying pan
Combed his hair with the leg of the chair
Dan Dan the funny wee man.

Can Can Caroline
Washed her hair in turpentine
Turpentine will make it shine
Can Can Caroline.

Keyhole Kate from the Gallowgate
Died last night at half past eight
They put her in a coffin
She fell through the bottom
Keyhole Kate from the Gallowgate.

Archibald bald bald
King of the jews jews jews
Bought his wife wife wife
A pair of shoes shoes shoes
When the shoes shoes shoes
Began to wear wear wear
Archibald bald bald
Began to swear swear swear
When the swear swear swear
Began to stop stop stop
Archibald bald bald
Bought a shop shop shop
When the shop shop shop
Began to sell sell sell
Archibald bald bald
Went to hell hell hell.

Up by the mountain
Down by the sea
Tommy broke a window
And he blamed it on me
Ah told ma ma
Ma ma told ma da
Tommy got a hammerin'
Ha Ha Ha.

Madamoiselle went into town V
Parlez vous
To buy herself a wedding gown
Parlez vous
And everybody in the town
Thought it was a lovely gown
Inky pinky parlez vous.

The big ship sails round the eely ally o
The eely ally o the eely ally o
The big ship sails round the eely ally o
On the last day of September
The captain says we'll have to go below
Have to go below, have to go below
The captain says we'll have to go below
On the last day of September.

The pillar box is red and fat
His mouth is very wide
He wears a tammy on his head
It must be dark inside
And really it's the greatest thrill
When mother lets me stop
And post the letters one by one
I love to hear them drop.

Bubble says the kettle
Bubble says the pot
Bubble bubble bubble
We are very hot
Shall I lift you off the fire
No you needn't trouble
That is just the way we talk
Bubble bubble bubble.

Miss Polly had a dolly
Who was sick sick sick
And she called for the doctor
To come quick quick quick
The doctor came with his bag and his hat
And he knocked at the door
With a rat tat tat
He looked at the dolly
And he shook his head
And he said Miss Polly
Put her straight to bed
He wrote out a letter for a pill pill pill
I'll be back in the morning
With a bill bill bill.

Where was Johnny when the lights went out?
Up Sauchiehall Street smokin' a doubt
The doubt was wee an' so was he
Where was Johnny when the lights went out?

Dial 999, dial 999,
Robert Beattie stole a sweetie
Dial 999!

"Vote vote vote for Annie Thomson"

46

Skipping Rope Rhymes

Skipping rope rhymes are sung whilst skipping with a skipping rope. If a child trips on the rope before the rhyme is finished she is 'out' and must start the rhyme again from the beginning.

Although a child can skip on her own with her own skipping rope it was more common to use a large rope (usually someone's old washing line) with a child at either end 'cawing' the rope for the others to jump. They were called the 'enders'.

If a child tripped on the rope or if her dress caught on the rope as she jumped out she was 'out' and must become an 'ender', the person whom she relieved would then be a jumper.

There were several ways to skip:

HIGH – The rope was cawed high above the ground and the child had to skip 'high'.

LOW – The rope was cawed with the enders on their hunkers (i.e. crouched bunny fashion) and the skipper would have to skip 'low'.

SLOW – The rope was cawed slowly and the skipper had to skip 'slow'.

MEDIUM – The rope was cawed not too fast and not too slow, just 'medium'.

ROCKY – The rope was rocked to and fro and the skipper had to jump backwards and forwards. ✓

HOPPY – The skipper had to skip on one leg only in a hopping fashion.

PEPPER – The rope was cawed as fast as the two enders could go and the skipper had to skip accordingly. ✓

Vote vote vote for Annie Thomson ✓
In comes Jeannie at the door
Jeannie is the one that we all love the best
And we don't want Annie any more.

There she goes there she goes
Peery heels and pointed toes
Look at her feet she thinks she's neat
Black stockins and dirty feet.

On a mountain stands a lady ✓
Who she is I do not know
All she wants is gold and silver
All she wants is a fine young man
So I call in Mary dear Mary dear Mary dear
So I call in Mary dear
And out pops Susie till the next new year.

Horsie horsie don't you stop ✓
Just let your feet go clippety clop
Your tail goes swish
And your wheels go round
Giddy up we're homeward bound.

I've a laudie in America
I've a laudie in Dundee i-ee i-ee
I've a laudie in Australia
And he's coming home to marry me i-ee i-ee
First he took me to America
Then he took me to Dundee i-ee i-ee
Then he ran away and left me
With three bonnie babies on my knee i-ee i-ee
One was sitting by the fireside
One was sitting on my knee i-ee i-ee
One was sitting at the doorstep
Crying daddy daddy daddy come to me i-ee i-ee.

A house to let apply within
A lady put out for drinking gin
Gin you know is a very bad thing
So out pops Mary and Annie comes in.

Pansy Potter the strong man's daughter
Went to school without her jotter
She got the belt began to cry
Pansy Potter said goodbye.

Christopher Columbus was a very brave man
He sailed o'er the ocean in an old tin can
And the waves grew higher and higher and over
One two three four five six
Seven eight nine ten out.

Elimination Rhymes

The elimination rhymes were used to see who would be 'Het' at a particular game, e.g. kick the can, hide and seek, tig, etc.

All the children would stand against a wall and the 'leader' would recite the rhyme and point to each child in turn as he spoke each word of the rhyme.

As the last word of the rhyme is spoken the child who is being pointed at is 'out'. The rhyme is then repeated with one child less eachhime. The child who is last 'out' is the one who is 'het'.

"Eeny meeny macka racka"

My mother and your mother
Were hanging out some clothes
My mother gave your mother
A punch on the nose
Guess what colour the blood will be
Close your eyes and think think think
Red (or blue, yellow, green, etc.)
R – E – D spells red
And red you must have on
If you have this colour on
Please step right out of this
G – A – M – E spells game
And O – U – T spells out
With a dirty washing clout
Right over your face
Just like that.

Eeny meeny macka racka
Em oh dominacka
Alla backa sugaracka
Om pom push.

One potato two potato three potato four
Five potato six potato seven potato more.

I think I think I smell a stink
Coming from Y – O – U.

53

There's a party on the hill
Will you come come come
Bring your own cup and saucer
And a bun bun bun
Mary will be there with a ribbon in her hair
Guess what colour the ribbon will be.
Red (or blue, yellow, green, etc.)
R – E – D spells red
And O – U – T spells out
With a dirty washing clout
Right over your face
Just like that.

Dic dic tation corporation
How many buses are in the station
Close your eyes and think of a lucky number
One two three etc.

Eeeny meeny miny mo
Catch a nipper by the toe
If he squeals let him go
Eeeny meeny miny mo.

Eeeny meeny miny mo
Sit the baby on the po
When he's done clean his bum
Eeeny meeny miny mo.

One two three four five six seven
All good children go to heaven
When they die their sins forgiven
One two three four five six seven.